Get Unstuck!

Companion Workbook

Copyright © 2024 Get Unstuck Media

Cover design by Olga Grlic
Typeset by Katalin Mélykuti
Marketing and distribution by Iva Sakan
Author picture by Patricia Vanrespaille

www.muriellemarie.com

ISBN: 9789464775235

Get Unstuck!

The ultimate guide to stop procrastinating and overthinking and finally move forward with your life and work.

Companion Workbook

Murielle Marie Ungricht

Table of Contents

The MOVE Method and How It Came to Life

"Those who do not move, do not notice their chains."
– Rosa Luxemburg

The MOVE method is a four-step process I created to help you get unstuck. It's based on thousands of coaching hours helping creatives and entrepreneurs figure out what they really want and support them in moving forward. In a private coaching series, I work one-on-one with clients and guide them through the process in a structured and intuitive way. I've chosen to follow the same structure in this book, adding background information, thinking prompts, philosophical theories, neuroscience discoveries, and coaching questions, as you move through the book.

The four steps of the method – Mindset, Options, Vision, and Execution – were always part of my work, but they've become more precise and were finetuned over the years. They combine what I learned by getting myself unstuck, what clients have shared with me that worked for them, and the many hours of work and experiments clients were willing to take on when working with me.

To gain the most from the method, I invite you to move through it step by step and follow along. Some parts might be familiar to you if you're familiar with the self-development process. I invite you not to skim over those parts but to use them as a reminder of your knowledge. Each step builds upon the previous one; they're stepping stones to a greater understanding of yourself, how getting unstuck works, and what you can do to get yourself moving again. Let's take a quick look at each step.

- **Mindset.** This step is about understanding what being stuck really means and how we get stuck. We're looking for clarity and awareness. We want to figure out what got you stuck and what keeps you there. What we think we can or cannot do – our mindset – is fundamental to getting unstuck. The exercises and thinking prompts will help you to gain more clarity about why you are where you are and help you to start figuring out how to get moving again.

- **Options.** Our minds can keep us trapped and stuck, which means that if we change our minds, we change our situation. This is the foundation of freedom: having options. Like most valuable things in life, freedom is not something other people will give you; it's something you must take for yourself. You do it by taking responsibility for your thoughts, emotions, and actions. A starting point to do that is looking at all the things you could be doing and all the opportunities available to you.

- **Vision.** It's great to figure out how your mind works and realize there's no limit to what you could be doing, having, or being. However, if you don't have a clear idea of which direction to go, it can still be challenging (not to say impossible) to see what is possible for you, make a choice, and take a step. That's why you need a vision for your life and your work. What is it that lights you up in the morning? What do you really want? What is truly important to you? In Step Three, we try to make sense of all these questions from a perspective of expansion and limitless possibilities.

- **Execution.** The final step of this book, work, and method is about taking action. Once you have a clear vision, you need to start implementing it in a way that feels good and is sustainable over time. This is where you put a plan together and take your first steps toward getting unstuck. I won't lie; this step requires courage, especially if you've been stuck for a while. Taking action will feel weird and icky.

But do not worry, I'll send you on your way with a few final tools to help you stay unstuck so you don't get lost or stranded right before reaching the finish line – or, should I say, the beginning of the rest of your wonderful life!

STEP ONE:
MINDSET

"All that we are is the result of what we have thought."
– Buddha

In this step, you'll learn:

- How to change your mindset by understanding how you think.
- The difference between a mindset that expands your reality and one that limits it.
- What it means to be stuck and how people get (and stay) stuck.
- The connection between being stuck and being afraid of change.
- The first step to getting unstuck and how change happens.
- That number one truth about life: everything always changes.
- How to embrace the messiness of change.

CHAPTER 1: WHAT IS MINDSET?

Our mindset dictates what we believe. It influences everything we think about, the way we feel, and, thus, the way we act. If we can shift our views, we can shift your mindset. But to do that, we first have to figure out what mindset we currently have: fixed or growth.

Fixed mindsets are static; these individuals believe what they believe, and there is no room for change. The world you see is immovable. Growth mindsets, on the other hand, believe that what they don't know can be learned. They know their skills, talents, and intelligence can be nurtured and grown.

The mindset you have will greatly impact how you see your world. The more positive and growth-oriented your mindset is, the happier and more successful you will be and the easier it will be to get yourself unstuck. Try the exercise below to see which type of mindset you have.

<u>Prompt: What type of mindset do you have?</u>   (Get Unstuck! paperback edition page 26)

Take a minute to think about this question. You can always choose to put pen to paper and write your answers down or think about them and answer them mentally as you read. Whatever works for you is fine.

How successful do you feel in what you undertake or want to accomplish?
To answer this question, look at how your life is organized. Your mindset is a determining factor, not only of the things you want to do but also of the things you're doing; it's essential to look at your life.

The most crucial point is this: your mindset influences your behavior. Your mindset is the driving force behind what you do, so it can restrict your actions, expand them, and make you take risks or not. Understanding this is huge!

Let's dig a little further. Look at the questions below, and answer them truthfully (nobody's watching, so don't worry, this is just for you!).

- **How is your mindset impacting your life?**
- **Do you think you have a fixed or a growth mindset?**

....

....

....

....

....

....

....

....

I know these are tough questions. Let's look at an example. Imagine you want to start something new: a creative project you think about a lot, a business you want to create, a change in your life that you know in your heart you must make, or any other idea that you can't seem to do anything about. Maybe...

- **you think you don't know how to start,**
- **you know you must do something about it, but you're waiting for the right time,**
- **you have no time to do it at all, so you keep postponing it,**
- **you're afraid of what will happen if you take a step,**
- **you started, but you fear you won't succeed,**
- **you... (fill in the blank).**

Whatever it is you're thinking, your mindset is what sets the tone. As a result, your mindset also drives your behavior and actions. That's precisely why it's so important to work on it.

If you've been feeling stuck, I guarantee you that your mindset plays a part in how you feel. Our mindset is one of the most important reasons we're not getting what we want out of life and achieving our goals. The truth is, there's nobody stopping us but our own thoughts. I know, it can be a hard pill to swallow, but it's true.

CHAPTER 2: WHAT DOES IT MEAN TO BE STUCK?

To understand how to get unstuck, we must first look at how we got stuck, what being stuck really means, and the complexity of getting started or moving forward.

What keeps us where we don't want to be is often a mix of practical considerations (overthinking and anxiety), emotional or mental blocks (inherited dreams or limiting beliefs, assumptions and opinions), and psychological factors (pain from the past or even trauma). Use the exercise below to assess where you are right now. When you want things to change, it's always good to know where you're starting from.

<u>Prompt: How stuck do you feel right now?</u>   (Get Unstuck! paperback edition page 31)

To know where we're going, it's essential to know where we're starting from. As a coach, one of the first questions I ask clients is where they are on the journey to achieving what they want. Nobody starts from nowhere. Whatever we're trying to accomplish, we usually have some tools already in our toolbox.

As you embark on this journey, it's essential to first get clear on what it is you're stuck on. We'll use this information as we progress through the book, so take a few minutes to reflect on what you want out of this experience.

Take a few deep breaths, ground yourself for a minute and then answer the following question, preferably on paper.

What are you stuck on right now? Be as specific as you can.

- **Is it a person, a place, a job, or a lifestyle that keeps you stuck?**
- **Does it have to do with finances, the place you live, and the people in your life?**
- **How does being stuck affect you? How does it make you feel?**
- **Have you tried making progress on a dream or goal for a while without success? What feels challenging about it?**
- **What area feels blocked when you think about your life or your work?**
- **If you weren't stuck, what would you be doing right now?**
- **If you weren't stuck, who would you be with? Where would you be?**
- **What would be different about your life or work if you could get unstuck right this minute?**

Feel free to add all the details you need to get a clear picture of where you are right now. The clearer that picture, the better we'll know how to work from where you are to where you want to be.

CHAPTER 4: THE MYTH OF CHANGE.

We tend to think about change as something that happens to us, rather than something we can control. While change might need a breaking point to ignite it, but in reality, we can light that match ourselves. All it takes is one small step, over and over. Try the exercise below to figure out what your ideal day, and therefore your ideal life, could be once you get unstuck.

<u>Prompt: Your ideal day and your ideal life</u>   (Get Unstuck! paperback edition page 61)

Give yourself some time to do this exercise. Pen and paper are great, but just thinking about it, in this case, is a form of doing too.

Imagine an ideal day. A day out of your beautiful, happy, and successful life. Not an out-of-the-ordinary day, so not a holiday, a day you run and win a marathon, or even your birthday – just a good, typical, happy day out of your ideal life.

When you have the image of this day in mind, start at the beginning when you open your eyes in the morning and let the day run its course until you get back into bed at night. Walk through your day mentally and look around you. What can you smell? What is hanging on the walls (if anything)? What can you hear, close by and in the distance? Let your imagination take you where it wants to go. This is not the moment to censor yourself (you've done enough of that already!). This is the moment to dream big.

As you're making your way through your ideal day, ask yourself:

- **What are you doing?**

What's the first thing you think about or do when you get up? Do you eat breakfast? If so, what's on your plate? Are you alone, or is someone with you? What do you feel? Do you stay in your pajamas or go straight to your closet to pick an outfit for the day? What happens afterward? How do you spend your morning? What do you have for lunch? What are you doing in the afternoon? Keep imagining your day until you go to bed at night, happy and inspired.

- **What do you see around you?**

When you open your eyes in the morning, what do you see around you? In what kind of room are you? Is there anything hanging on the walls? When you step out of the bedroom or where you slept, what does the place you call "home" look like? Are you in a villa, a house, an apartment? Are you sliding open the door of the campervan you're touring around the country with? Are you living in a cabin in the middle of nature? Are you lounging on a beach with a mocktail or sitting inside at a desk? How does your day feel? How's the weather? What do you hear in the distance? What's happening around you?

- **Where is your attention going?**

What are you focused on? Are you working, writing, or on a video call with someone? Cooking something delicious for the kids who are about to come home? What are your thoughts? Is there something in the back of your mind, something you can't forget, like a birthday or a deadline for an important project?

- **How are you feeling?**

How's your body feeling? Is there tension somewhere, or are you relaxed and chill? What emotions are you experiencing? How's your heart doing? How are your lungs? Are you hot or cold? Are you happy? Is there something you look forward to? If you had to pick one thing, what would you say is the most beautiful part of your day?

- **What about your ideal life?**

Stringing beautiful days like the one you just imagined together creates an ideal life. What would you need to add to the day you just described to turn it into a life you could genuinely enjoy living? What should you have, do and be to live out your most beautiful life? How could you start gently adding some of that into your life today?

CHAPTER 5: HOW DOES CHANGE HAPPEN?

Getting unstuck requires that we take back control of how and when we make changes. Now that you've imagined a day in the life you could be living, you have an idea of how to make real change happen. Unfortunately, this is usually the point where your inner voice starts whispering why this new life – this change – will never happen or that you're not good enough.

Let's shut that voice down with the exercise below.

<u>Prompt: What do you want to do with the rest of your life?</u>   (Get Unstuck! paperback edition page 65)

We don't know what our lives will ultimately be made of or how long we have to live. This is a mystery and insecurity we must all live with. Many philosophers throughout history spent their lives trying to solve the riddle of a life well lived. It's not an easy nut to crack, and I don't claim I will do that here. But I firmly believe that you should not waste the precious life you've been given. Every day spent being stuck is a day you'll never get back. To get over the fear of change, it helps to remind yourself of how little time you have and how important the decisions you make are.

- **How long do you have left?**

I'm in my forties as I'm writing these words. Going by averages for females living in Europe, I guess I have about the same number of years left as I've already lived. Forty-something years doesn't sound too bad, does it? At the same time, I'm more than halfway through, which, without wanting to sound morbid, is a lot. Of the 4000 weeks I approximately have, I've already spent about 2400. This means I have 1600 weeks left. Luckily, the years I've lived have taught me many interesting (and sometimes painful) lessons. Hopefully, moving forward, I'll be smarter with my time and how I decide to spend it. How about you? How old are you? And how much time do you have left? When you've answered the question, stay with it for a few minutes and feel what that means to you and your dreams.

- **What do you want your life to look like from this moment on?**

Go back to the Ideal Day and Ideal Life exercise and review your answers. When you're done, answer the questions below without too much overthinking. Just allow what comes up.

- **What do you want to experience?**
- **What kind of person do you want to be?**
- **How do you want to feel?**
- **What impact do you want to have on the world?**
- **Who do you want to be with?**
- **What do you want to learn or know?**
- **How are you going to live your life from this day forward?**

CHAPTER 6: IMPERMANENCE IS THE ONLY TRUTH.

Our sense of self, our wish to understand the world as it unfolds before us, intuitively works against the reality that nothing is permanent. Our mind loves giving meaning to the things we see and experience and constantly creates systems and structures of understanding. While this characteristic helps us live, set goals, and achieve the things we want, it also tricks us into believe that we are somehow at the center of something.

Try the thought experiment below to see how this mindset can affect your life.

<u>Prompt: Does everything really stay the same?</u>   (Get Unstuck! paperback edition page 71)

For this thought experiment, take a few deep breaths, come into the present moment, and look around you for a few minutes.

Take in what you see, what you hear, and what you feel. Look at the objects around you, what you're sitting or lying down on, and your clothes. Feel the textures surrounding you, the book you're holding in your hands, or looking at on a screen somehow. Now try to feel the permanence of this moment. Ask yourself the following questions:

- **Will everything I see, touch, and hold in my hands still be here tomorrow?**
- **Will all of what I see around me still exist tomorrow?**
- **Will anything about me or what surrounds me be different when I wake up?**

Now project yourself into the future. Not a month, a year, or a decade, but fifty or a hundred years from now. Take a number that feels big for you. One you believe you won't be around to see. When you have that number in your mind, answer the following questions:

- **Will everything I see, touch, and hold in my hands still be here (your number) years from now?**
- **Will all I see around me still exist (your number) years from now?**
- **If I were to wake up (your number) years from now, would anything about me or what surrounds me be different?**

STEP TWO: OPTIONS

In this step, you'll learn:

- That the world is full of possibilities, you just need to see them for it to be so.
- That you're the leader of your life.
- What the tyranny of inherited dreams is and how it influences your life.
- How outdated ideas of success keep most people stuck.
- How our environment shapes our reality.
- That getting unstuck is not only about seeing, but also about creating new possibilities for yourself.

CHAPTER 1: COMING HOME TO YOURSELF.

Society has imposed on us their dreams. I call them "inherited dreams." But there's something else buried beneath those inherited dreams: our truest, most authentic dreams.

We all have authentic dreams. The problem is that most of us don't know what we want because other people's dreams cloud our judgment. Finding your way back to your dreams means taking leadership in your life. In the exercises below, we will search for our authentic dreams by going back to our childhood selves.

<u>Prompt: Your Childhood Self</u>   (Get Unstuck! print edition page 92)

This activity will help you to remember who you are and what makes you happy. To do that, I want you to tap into your deeper essence and remember your earliest dreams and wishes. Find a quiet place to sit down and write, relax, take a deep breath, and think about the questions below and what they bring up for you.

Think back to your childhood memories. Quietly listen.

- **What did you want to be when you were a child?**
- **What made you the happiest?**
- **What were you good at?**
- **What did you enjoy doing?**
- **How did you love spending your time?**

What do you see when you think back about that little human and all that they loved to do and dream about? Who might you have become if your childhood self had followed their dreams?

Write down ten things you loved to do as a child. Next to each one, write down if you still love or would love to do that now. Then, for each item, write down the last time you did it.

Are these things still part of your life? Do you miss them? Do you want them in your life again?

Prompt: Tapping into Your Deeper Knowing   (Get Unstuck! paperback edition page 96)

With this activity, I want you to tap into the parts of you that are often ignored. Because of the intensity of this exercise, your inner critic might show up. If this happens, know that it's not uncommon for your mind to want to protect you from your authentic dreams. They're the ones that matter most, so there will be some resistance. By staying close to your center – breathing deeply, remembering why you picked up this book, and focusing on how important it is for you to get unstuck, you'll be able to counteract those thoughts and move forward. Whatever your inner voice says!

Read through the questions below. Answer the ones that speak to you (remember: it's okay to skip anything that isn't right for you, leadership starts with making your own choices).

- **What do you currently do, or have done, that makes you feel your happiest?**
- **If you had the right education or skill set, you'd definitely try ____________, because ____________.**
- **What personal attitude, skill, or attribute are you proud of?**
- **What was something (person, book, movie, quote, and so on) that inspired you in the last year? Why?**
- **Is your dream career (from when you were younger) different from what you're doing now? Does it look anything like what you thought it would? In what ways?**
- **Was there an event, moment, or feeling this past year where your gut, instinct, or heart spoke to you somehow? What happened, and what do you think it means?**
- **Was there an event or moment where you felt confident, happy, and joyful? When was it, and what were you doing?**

After answering the questions, please read them, examine them from a place of curiosity and wonder, and highlight any themes, patterns, or thoughts that stand out. These themes point to what your childhood self (or true self) is trying to tell you.

CHAPTER 2: LEADERSHIP IS NEVER GIVEN, YOU HAVE TO TAKE IT FOR YOURSELF.

To get unstuck, we must be willing to dig deep and see the mud sticking to our boots, preventing us from getting out of the wetlands. It's called leadership. We must admit to ourselves that we're the one staying in the mire and that we have a role to play in getting ourselves out of there. It's up to us.

Personal leadership is about examining our lives and actions and questioning the rules we live by. We need to be a participant in our lives, not a bystander. We need to actively choose our behavior and acknowledge that our behavior shapes our environment. To ensure we are choosing the behaviors that will help us get unstuck, we have to make sure our environment is working for us.

Try this exercise to see how your environment is affecting your behavior and how you can change it to better reflect what you want out of life and work.

<u>Prompt: Design your environment for success</u> (Get Unstuck! paperback edition page 110)

Look around you at home, work (or your home office), and think of the spaces you regularly frequent, like the grocery store, the gym, etc. Now consider your goals and answer the following questions:

- **Is my home environment supporting me in making decisions aligned with my goals?**

Imagine you want to read more and watch fewer videos on demand in the evenings. Is your environment encouraging you to do that? How easy is it to turn on a show on your smartphone or television versus picking up a book and reading? How could you make your environment more encouraging for the good behavior or habit you want to have?

- **Is my work environment supporting me in making decisions aligned with my goals?**

Think of your place of work, your desk, and how your work environment is organized. Is this environment helping you do your work positively, or is it making it harder for you to focus and do what you need to do? How could you change your environment, so it encourages better work from you?

- **Are the spaces I frequent helping me to achieve my goals?**

Let's say you aim to eat more vegetables and cook one meat-free meal every week, but this is a challenging lifestyle change for you. Is your grocery store of choice placing a hurdle between you and the behavior you want to change, or is it encouraging it? How could you change that so it becomes easier to stick to your meat-free day once a week?

Once you've reviewed the spaces you spend time in regularly, come up with three things you can do to make your environment work for you. Remember: your environment has to align with your goals – if it isn't, you'll have to use willpower to get anything done, a finite resource that you'd better not bet your dreams on.

CHAPTER 3: WHAT DO YOU REALLY WANT?

In truth, we all know what we want. We might not have the specifics or details aligned, but we know what direction we want to take, and we definitely know what don't want to do anymore. In the exercise below, we'll get a better idea of what our true desires really are.

<u>Prompt: What do you really want?</u>　　　(Get Unstuck! paperback edition page 113)

Close your eyes, take a deep breath, and be honest with yourself for a few moments. Think about your life, work, relationships, and yourself... Feel into who you are and what matters to you most. Get to the core of your being; touch your soul. Stay there for a few minutes and be open and curious about what wants to come up. Then ask yourself the following questions:

- **What do I "know" I want to do or should be doing to be happy?**
- **What would I "like" to do but think I won't be capable of?**
- **What have I "always wanted" to do but keep telling myself won't work out?**

Reflect on these questions for a few moments, so you can hear what your intuition and gut are telling you before your inner critic takes over. Take a (mental) note; we'll return to this later.

PS: If you can't come up with anything, don't worry. At this stage, it's not abnormal for your dreams and desires to be blocked, especially if you've been following other people's dreams for a long time. If this is you, I invite you to lean into the idea that "the goal might just be to have a dream." It's a great starting point to help you get unstuck.

CHAPTER 4: OPPORTUNITIES SHOW UP
WHEN YOU MAKE ROOM FOR THEM

Getting unstuck is not just about seeing new possibilities, but about creating new possibilities for ourselves. We need to remove the blindfold, see where we want to be going, and then take the steps to get there.

In the exercise below, I want you to imagine the opportunities that are around you.

<u>Prompt: Look at your life with new eyes</u>   (Get Unstuck! paperback edition page 121)

To see new opportunities, you need to remove the blindfold. A good starting point is to look at your life with the eyes of a beginner, someone who doesn't know anything about your life or who you are. Imagine you're someone else, someone you appreciate or that you look up to. Now, look at yourself through that person's eyes. Take the facts, look at what you see around yourself, and start there.

- **What are you doing?**
- **Where are you?**
- **Who's with you?**
- **What are you famous for?**
- **What options are available to you?**

Take some time to reflect on your answers. What new opportunities emerge when you look at yourself from the outside this way? Write them down.

CHAPTER 5: REAL-LIFE EXPERIMENTS TO ACTIVATE CHANGE.

To get unstuck, we must take action. We have to go out and try things, experiment with things. We can't just think ourselves out of being stuck. Unfortunately, if our experiences teach us that we can't do something, then our unconscious thoughts and beliefs will convince us we can't do it. However, if we examine our worldview, debunk our false beliefs, and review the theories and rules that we've learned from them, and thus live by, we can activate change.

Try the exercise below to learn more about the beliefs that are keeping us stuck.

<u>Prompt: The beliefs that keep you stuck right now</u>   (Get Unstuck! paperback edition page 129)

With this final activity of Step Two of this book, I want you to look deeper at your beliefs. It's a continuation of the inner critic exercise you did earlier, but it's different. Previously, you uncovered the negative thoughts that keep you stuck. Now we want to take it a step further: we want to dig up the beliefs about yourself and your situation that keep you stuck.

Take a deep breath, and either on paper or in your mind, reflect on the following questions:

- **If I'm honest with myself, what is the #1 thing holding me back right now?**
- **What do I believe will happen if I do what I know deep down I want to do?**
- **What doom scenarios am I making up in my head when I think about this change?**
- **How much of this doom scenario might actually come true? How do I know for sure?**
- **Do I care what other people will say if I do what I really want to do? What do I believe they will say?**
- **What is so wrong with what I want to do that I'm not allowing myself to do it?**

These questions are tough, I know, so take your time. Once you've uncovered the beliefs that keep you stuck right now, I want you to ask yourself the following two questions:

- How much of myself am I denying by staying where I am because of these beliefs?
- What will my life be like five years from now if I let myself be guided by these beliefs?

STEP THREE: VISION

"Find out who you are and do it on purpose."
– Dolly Parton

In this step, you'll learn:

- That it's ok to be different, and how to turn your difference(s) into an advantage.
- Why breaking promises to yourself will keep you stuck.
- Why real impostors don't feel like impostors.
- Disruptive strategies and how they can help you get unstuck.
- How we make perceptual judgments, and why most of them are false.
- How to change and influence your reality.

CHAPTER 1: WHO DO YOU WANT TO BE WHEN YOU GROW UP?

We focus so much on belonging that we don't see the differences between ourselves and the group we want to belong to. Instead, we desperately try to become like them, believing it is the only way we will succeed in life. We think that if we just work a little harder, try a little more, we'll finally be the same as everyone else, and that will lead to life-long happiness.

The reality is, the longer we try to fit a square peg into a round hole, the longer we stay stuck. It's only when we accept that we're different that positive changes can happen, and the vision of the life we're meant to have can emerge.

<u>Prompt: Are you someone with many ideas and interests?</u>   (Get Unstuck! paperback edition page 144)

The more I do this work, the more I realize there are a lot of creative generalists out there: people with many ideas and interests who don't fit into the tiny box of specialization that the world is trying to put them in. The questions below can guide you to figure out if you're part of that fantastic crew of incredible swans (the fact that you're still with me tells me that you might!).

- **Do you get bored quickly when you figure out how something works, how to do it, or if you have to do the same thing too often?**
- **Do you enjoy learning, researching, exploring, and developing new skills or insights?**
- **Do you keep changing your mind about what you want to do with your life? Are you still wondering what you'll be when you "grow up"?**
- **Is it difficult for you to explain to someone what you do?**
- **Do you often daydream about everything you "still" want to do or will do "someday," both professionally and personally?**
- **Do you start many things but often only finish a few of them?**
- **Do you feel like you need to be more focused?**
- **Do you have trouble choosing for fear of losing something?**
- **Is there a rebel living inside of you that hates authority and can't stand injustice?**

If you answered "yes" to three or more of the questions above, there's a good chance that you're a creative generalist.

CHAPTER 2: THE BURDEN OF BEING UNCONVENTIONAL.

The things we tell ourselves shape what we believe is possible. Our beliefs then influence our behavior, keeping us stuck. The more negative self-talk we do, and the more we care about what others think, the smaller our vision of what is possible stays.

The exercise below will help you take stock of the limits you've placed on what is possible for you.

<u>Prompt: The limits you place on yourself</u>   (Get Unstuck! paperback edition page 158)

First, find a quiet place and make yourself comfortable. Take pen and paper if you like. Once you feel centered and calm, answer the following questions:

- **Have you ever felt like you didn't belong? When did it start? What beliefs did it create in you? Are those beliefs still influencing your life? If so, how?**
- **Do you feel shame and guilt at times? Are these feelings holding you back from doing things you want to do? In your personal, professional life, or both?**
- **Think about keeping promises to yourself; what comes to mind? Do you sometimes break promises to yourself? How could you deal with what you promise yourself in the future? How might that impact or change your life?**
- **Do you sometimes feel like an impostor? Do you have a strong urge to prove yourself? When do you feel like an impostor the most? And what exactly do you want to prove? To whom?**
- **When you think about what you want, what's the voice in your head telling you? How is what that voice says impacting your vision? Is that voice keeping you small or helping you grow?**
- **What would you do if you allowed yourself to dream? If you felt okay with being unconventional or different. Who would you be? What would you change about your life?**
- **What's holding you back? What's keeping you stuck? Be honest with yourself; nobody's watching. It's just you, so be brave and give yourself the gift of absolute truth.**

CHAPTER 3: DISRUPTIVE STRATEGIES

Consciously trying to solve a significant life or work question without tapping into your intuition is like trying to climb Mount Everest with some Home Depot rope and a kitchen knife. When you are faced with a non-acute problem, tapping into your intuition requires a calm mind, room to breathe and think, and a bit of letting go. But to figure out what our intuition is trying to tell us, we first have to learn how to tap into it.

Prompt: Tapping into your intuition to help you get unstuck (Get Unstuck! paperback edition page 171)

Make yourself comfortable. When you feel centered and calm, bring what you're stuck on into your mind. Stay focused on it for a little while and look at it from different perspectives:

- How long have you felt this way or thought about this?
- What have you tried in the past?
- What do you believe about this?
- Where/how do you feel stuck the most?
- What would success look like for this?

Feel into what this problem (question, decision, change you want to make, or anything else that's keeping you stuck) does with your body:

- **Where in your body are you feeling the stuckness?**
- **What sensations are you experiencing when you're thinking about being stuck?**
- **What is happening to your heart rate, breathing, and skin?**

Once you're in tune with your mind and body, close your eyes and let your intuition take over. Make sure not to analyze, question, or invalidate what comes up. That's how we're trained to let our analytical mind silence our intuition:

- **What images and symbols come up? Let yourself dive into them fully.**
- **What concepts, ideas, and options feel right in your body?**
- **What do you feel, sense, hear, and perceive? Allow all of it.**
- **If you've been pondering a yes or no choice, what feels right in your body?**
- **When you're thinking about what you could do to move forward, do you have an open or closed sensation in your body? Open is your intuition, a feeling of I want to, while closed is often fear, ego, or any other limits you place on yourself from the realm of I have to.**

As I've said before, we cannot think ourselves into a new life or career. We have to take action. We must go out and do it. And in order to do that, we need to let go of what we think might happen and take on a new perspective.

<u>Prompt: How do you talk yourself out of your dreams?</u> (Get Unstuck! paperback edition page 177)

This is an important question, especially if you've felt stuck for a while. In Step Two, I asked you to think about the beliefs that keep you stuck. This exercise builds on that. Feel free to revisit that exercise before moving forward with this one.

When you're ready, take a deep breath and think of how stuck you feel right now. Picture what or who you believe is not allowing you to move forward. When you have that picture, go through the statements below. For each, ask yourself if you've ever had or currently have comparable thoughts or feelings regarding your situation. Be specific.

- **If this happened to someone else, I would know what they should do, and I would tell them! But when it comes to me, I simply don't know what to do.**
- **I've tried everything. I've also thought about everything. But whatever I try or think, nothing ever gets me unstuck. I've been feeling like this forever.**
- **There's so much I could do; the problem is, I don't know what to do precisely. From all the options that I have, what is the project I should pick?**
- **I have no choice. I've tried to get out of this situation, but there's just nothing I can do about it.**
- **Everyone I meet wants to help me with advice. The problem is, that advice might work for them, but it certainly won't work for me.**
- **What if I make the wrong decision? I know what I have now but not what I'll get. Whenever I think about doing something, I get scared I will end up in a gutter somewhere.**
- **Everything looks too big. It's so overwhelming that I feel completely paralyzed and don't know where to start. I want to do something but I just don't know what.**

Take note of the statements that sound familiar to you. If these or similar ones pop up in your mind regularly, you might be suffering from a mix of confirmation bias (see below) and the opportunity blindness we talked about in Step Two. It's not that you don't have options to choose from; you're just not seeing them. Let's fix that, shall we?

CHAPTER 4: CONFIRMATION BIAS AND MOTIVATED REASONING.

As we experience something, our brain and senses are interpreting it for us. However, a lot can go wrong in that interpretation phase, causing us to react to our experiences in a certain way. This is why siblings can have the same experiences as one another but have vastly different memories – or interpretations – of the experience.

This means that if we acknowledge that our reality is subjective (because it is influenced by our brain and senses interpretation of it), then we can change it by reinterpreting it. The exercise below will walk you through how to recognize what your perspective is on certain things and how it differs from someone else's.

<u>Prompt: My perspective versus that of other people</u>   (Get Unstuck! paperback edition page 185)

Think about what you're stuck on and think back to the answers you gave in the previous exercise: how you talk yourself out of your dreams. Take a few moments to ground yourself, then answer the following:

- What is my perspective on being stuck?
- What is the view of someone that loves me that I've spoken to about this problem?
- What is the attitude of my family members?
- What would the perspective of someone I admire be on why I'm stuck?
- What would the perspective of my favorite high school teacher be?
- What would the view of my least favorite person in the world be?

Once you've answered the questions above, combine them into a broader and more encompassing perspective about your situation. Go back to the second prompt from Step One: How stuck do you feel right now? and review what you wrote.

- **Is there anything that pops out?**
- **What is now true about why you're stuck that wasn't true (or visible to you) before?**
- **What new perspectives and/or opportunities have emerged?**
- **How can this help you get unstuck?**

CHAPTER 6: INSIGHTS, ENLIGHTENMENT, AND GETTING UNSTUCK.

Disruption gives us insights into our lives that can enlighten us about what we want out of our lives.

In Step Two, I asked you to reflect on what you really want. Go back and read your answer. In light of what you've learned, answer the question again: **What do you really want?**
(Get Unstuck! print edition page 200)

STEP FOUR: EXECUTION

"All progress begins with a brave decision. Action comes before the courage to act. Action generates motivation."
- Marie Forleo

In this step, you'll learn:

- That trying everything is as bad as trying nothing.
- How to not get overwhelmed by the choices that you have.
- The power of valued living versus achievement-based living.
- How you might be using every excuse in the book to not change.
- The truth about fear and how to not let it stop you from doing what you want.
- The impact of trauma and childhood wounds on being and staying stuck.
- What your glue is and how you can use it to make sense of your life.
- The myth of willpower and the paradox of choice.
- Three strategies to stay unstuck.

CHAPTER 1: IF YOU'RE LOOKING FOR FLAWS, YOU'LL FIND THEM.

We always start to get untuck before we think we do. The problem is, we immediately look for thee flaws and talk ourselves out of taking action. We get stuck in a cycle of trying things, but never stick to one thing long enough to see how its benefitting us. There is a lack of consistency. Instead, we are looking for a quick fix.

You need to remember that creating the life and work of your dreams is a lifelong process, and each step taken consciously will guide you closer to that goal. With the exercise below, I want you to think about all the ways you've tried to get unstuck before.

Prompt: How did you try to get unstuck in the past?   (Get Unstuck! paperback edition page 209)

Here are a few questions to help you filter out successful strategies that helped you achieve your goals in the past. On paper or mentally, take some time to review them and answer them as truthfully as you can (nobody's watching, just be honest with yourself).

- **Think of your successes and failures. What was different about how you chose the goals you achieved and those that you didn't? What was different in how you tried to achieve them?**
- **Were you clear on your desires? How did it affect the success or failure of your goals?**
- **What would you do differently now to try to change something about yourself, your life, or your work?**
- **Did you choose your goals freely, or were you going after inherited dreams? How did this affect your progress and success?**
- **Anything else you think influenced your success or failure?**

____

____

____

____

____

____

____

____

____

____

____

____

____

____

Getting unstuck is a process of unraveling, imagination, and creation. It starts with discovering more about ourselves and what we want.

We all operate with an internal set of values. The problem is our inherited dreams bury those internal values beneath false beliefs and societal expectations. In the exercise below, you'll identify your five core values.

<u>Prompt: Identifying the values that speak to you.</u> (Get Unstuck! paperback edition page 215)

This exercise aims to identify the values you feel connected to intuitively, not those you've inherited or been conditioned to identify with. Below is a list of values. Read through the list, and circle or write down all the values that speak to you. If you possess some values that aren't on the list, feel free to add as many as you like. Try to do this as a free-flow exercise without overthinking why you choose particular values over others.

Abundance	Enjoyment	Performance
Acceptance	Entertainment	Perseverance
Accomplishment	Enthusiasm	Persistence

Accountability
Accuracy
Achievement
Activity
Adaptability
Advancement
Adventure
Advocacy
Affection
Agility
Alertness
Altruism
Ambition
Amusement
Appreciation
Approachability
Assertiveness
Attentiveness
Attractiveness
Autonomy
Availability
Awareness
Balance
Beauty
Belonging
Benevolence
Boldness
Bravery
Brilliance
Calmness
Candor
Capability
Carefulness
Caring
Certainty
Challenge
Change
Charity
Cheerfulness
Cleanliness
Cleverness
Collaboration
Comfort

Entrepreneurship
Environment
Equality
Equitability
Ethics
Excellence
Excitement
Experience
Expertise
Exploration
Expressiveness
Extrovert
Exuberance
Fairness
Faithfulness
Family
Fearlessness
Feelings
Fidelity
Fierce
Firm
Flexibility
Flow
Focus
Foresight
Forgiveness
Fortitude
Freedom
Friendships
Frugality
Fun
Generosity
Genius
Gentleness
Giving
Goodness
Grace
Gratitude
Greatness
Growth
Guidance
Happiness
Hard work

Philanthropy
Playfulness
Popularity
Positivity
Potential
Power
Practicality
Pragmatism
Presence
Proactivity
Productivity
Professionalism
Progress
Prudence
Punctuality
Purity
Purpose
Quality
Radiance
Rationality
Receptiveness
Recognition
Reflection
Relationships
Reliability
Resilience
Resourcefulness
Respect
Responsibility
Responsiveness
Restraint
Reverence
Rigor
Risk Taking
Sacrifice
Safety
Satisfaction
Security
Self Awareness
Self-Reliance
Selflessness
Sensitivity
Sensuality

Commitment	Harmony	Serenity
Common sense	Health	Seriousness
Communication	Heart	Sharing
Community	Helpfulness	Significance
Compassion	Heroism	Silence
Competency	Honesty	Silliness
Completion	Honor	Simplicity
Concentration	Hope	Sincerity
Concern for Others	Humility	Skillfulness
Confidence	Humor	Softness
Conformity	Imagination	Solitude
Connection	Impact	Spirituality
Consciousness	Impartiality	Spontaneity
Consistency	Inclusiveness	Stability
Contentment	Independence	Status
Contribution	Individuality	Strength
Control	Innovation	Structure
Conviction	Insightfulness	Success
Cooperation	Inspiration	Support
Courage	Integrity	Sustainability
Courtesy	Intelligence	Sympathy
Craftiness	Intensity	Synergy
Creativity	Introspection	Talent
Credibility	Intuition	Teamwork
Curiosity	Inviting	Temperance
Daring	Joy	Tenderness
Decisiveness	Justice	Thankfulness
Dedication	Kindness	Thoughtfulness
Delight	Knowledge	Tolerance
Dependability	Leadership	Traditionalism
Depth	Learning	Tranquility
Determination	Listening	Transparency
Development	Liveliness	Trustworthiness
Devotion	Logic	Truth
Dignity	Longevity	Understanding
Diligence	Love	Uniqueness
Directness	Loyalty	Usefulness
Discipline	Making a difference	Value
Discovery	Meaning	Versatility
Diversity	Merit	Virtue
Down-to-Earth	Meticulousness	Vision
Dreaming	Mindfulness	Vitality
Drive	Moderation	Vulnerability

Duty	Modesty	Warmth
Eagerness	Motivation	Wealth
Education	Mystery	Welcoming
Effectiveness	Nurturing	Well-Being
Efficiency	Obedience	Willfulness
Elegance	Open-Mindedness	Wisdom
Emotionality	Openness	Wonder
Empathy	Optimism	Zeal
Empowerment	Originality	
Encouragement	Passion	
Endurance	Patience	
Energy	Peace	
Engagement	Perfection	

Use the outer circles of the diagram below to group your core values in a way that makes sense. This could be based on what they represent to you, a particular category of values, or anything else that makes them stand out as a group for you. Once you're done, pick the most important one from each group and write it in the center of the diagram. Those are your five core values. Congratulations!

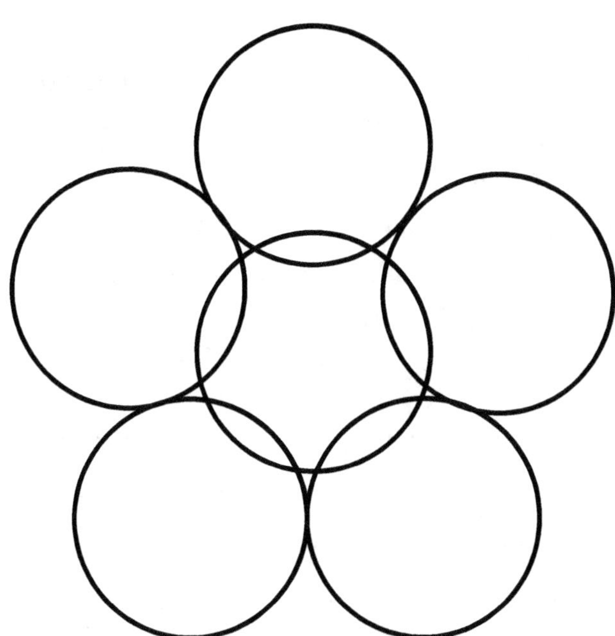

Write them down on a piece of paper in order of importance (the most important one at the top), and put your list somewhere visible so you can have your five core values close by when you need them as a reminder of what you stand for. I have mine hanging on my office wall, but you can also stick them in your planner, bag, or purse. Whatever works best for you.

CHAPTER 2: USING EVERY EXCUSE IN THE BOOK NOT TO CHANGE.

There are four types of people who get stuck: the ones who do nothing because they have too many choices and get overwhelmed, the ones you try everything but never stick to anything long enough to make it work, the ones who immediately find flaws in their ideas and talk themselves out of doing them, and the ones who use every excuse they can find not to change.

The fear of losing something, of admitting we aren't perfect, or of actively changing our realities is terrifying. So, instead of pushing past that fear, we let it hold us more firmly in place.

To stop making excuses, we must realize that we control our destinies. We can make the choice to take action and live a more intentional life. But how do we stop making excuses and take those necessary steps?

<u>Prompt: Stop making excuses for yourself.</u>   (Get Unstuck! paperback edition page 222)

If you often find yourself coming up with excuses for not pushing an idea forward, or the next time you're tempted to give up because you came up with a perfect excuse not to do something, try addressing the reasons you're coming up with by asking yourself the following questions:

- **Is this thought realistic? Is it really true?**
- **Is this excuse valid? Would I believe it if someone else was saying this to me?**
- **Why am I afraid of moving forward? What is fear trying to tell me?**
- **What's the worst that can happen?**
- **If I listen to this excuse and do nothing, what will happen?**
- **What will happen if I don't listen to this excuse and take action?**
- **Do I really want to change?**
- **What is my next step here?**

____

____

____

____

____

____

____

____

____

____

<u>Prompt: Identifying the values that speak to you.</u>   (Get Unstuck! paperback edition page 238)

Now that you've gained insights about all the tricks your unconscious mind can play on you to keep you stuck, go back to your answer to the question "What do you really want?" and review what came up.

Then, to list your dreams, goals, and desires, ask yourself these questions:

- Are there other options available that I didn't consider before?
- Is this really what I want? Am I keeping my desires small, or am I going all in?
- Am I making excuses for myself?
- Am I talking myself out of the things I want by finding flaws in everything?
- Is what I want realistic? (Eg. Can I become an astronaut at 37?) If not, what could I do instead? And what do I really like about the idea of being an astronaut?
- Is perfectionism making my dreams impossible?
- Am I staying where I am because I've already invested a lot in this relationship, career, etc.?
- Is this dream important enough to me that I do everything to achieve it?
- What is the first step to making this my new reality?
- How am I going to keep myself accountable and motivated?
- What am I missing to go after this dream?

....

....

....

....

....

....

....

....

....

....

....

....

CHAPTER 3: FEAR ITSELF.

We create and life out self-fulfilling prophecies. Every day we live up to our self-image, we act as the person we think we are, and so we become that person. If we want to change, we must tell ourselves a different story. This includes our relationship to fear. When our internal dialogue is really fear voicing its opinion, it stops us from taking action. Learning to decipher the voice of fear from our intuition, is a huge part of getting us unstuck.

To recognize what fears are holding us back and why, I want you to try the following exercise.

<u>Prompt: Whenever fear is holding you back, do this.</u>   (Get Unstuck! paperback edition page 243)

- **Review your fears**

A powerful question that has helped many clients and I is: "What's the worst that can happen?" Whenever you experience fear, ask yourself this question and write down everything you can think of. When your list is ready, review the items and try to identify the worst outcome. Now compare that worst outcome with the life you'll have if you don't pursue your passion, goals or dreams.

- **Embrace your fears**

After you realize that your worst outcome is probably much better than the unhappiness and unfulfilled life ahead of you if you don't follow your dreams, accept that answering your calling is scary. That's okay and something we all experience. This is why befriending and accepting your fears is so powerful, especially when undertaking new and exciting things.

- **Transform your fears**

A great way to live with your fears and make them work for you is to channel them into something empowering. Transform your negative thoughts into positive mantras that you repeat to yourself daily, and your fears will change in your favor. It might be something as simple as starting to say "I can" instead of "I can't" or "yes, why not?" instead of "no, not me." A mantra that has helped me many times to move through fear is: "it's not dangerous, it's old programming." I use it whenever I feel fear or anxiety taking over, especially when I'm about to do something bold and new. Reminding myself that it's a reaction of my nervous system to the past helps to stay grounded and focused in the present (where there is no danger!).

- **Avoid letting fear shut you down**

Whatever you do when you experience fear, please take action and do whatever it takes to avoid shutting down. The simplest way to accomplish this is to sit with your fears and "do it anyway." There's no easy way to do this except through practice. However, by using fear as a trigger, you'll diffuse it from the start, and it will get easier.

- **Don't let fear guide you**

I'll be the first to admit that fear is very powerful. If left alone and free to play games with your mind, fear will eventually lead you away from your dreams and desires, cloud your judgment, and drag you down. The first step to avoiding this happening is recognizing your fears and knowing when they try to lead you. Awareness of your thoughts, feelings, and emotions will help you stand against fear and not let it guide you.

- **Prevent fear from deciding for you**

Fear is not only powerful, but it's also very deceiving. If a fear stays with you long enough and you don't challenge it, it will become part of your belief system. When this happens, fear starts to dictate your decisions and give direction to your life. Prevent fears from becoming familiar by habitually questioning your belief system and turning inwards. Doing this is essential to know what makes you happy and give your life the direction you want.

As I shared while rocking a Blondie t-shirt on a TEDx stage a few years ago, we should never believe anything we think – at least not without questioning our thoughts first. It's one of the biggest reasons we don't achieve our goals. Instead, we should prove our inner voice wrong by taking action over fear.

It's important to remember that being ready is not a feeling, it is a decision. Mel Robbins talks about this in her Tedx talk from 2013, *How to stop screwing yourself over*, and in her book *The 5 Second Rule*. I've shared it with so many people and watched them benefit from it. I'd love for you to try it.

<u>Prompt: The 5 Second Rule (by Mel Robbins)</u>   (Get Unstuck! paperback edition page 250)

Whenever you feel like you're talking yourself out of an idea, try Mel Robbins' 5-Second Rule. This American Lawyer turned self-help author, and motivational speaker explained how the rule works in her book, *The 5 Second Rule*. It goes like this:

"The 5 Second Rule is simple. If you have an instinct to act on a goal, you must physically move within 5 seconds or your brain will kill it. The moment you feel an instinct or a desire to act on a goal or a commitment, use the Rule. (...) When you feel yourself hesitate before doing something that you know you should do, count 5-4-3-2-1-GO and move towards action."

CHAPTER 4: TRAUMA AND CHILDHOOD WOUNDS.

Connecting with our inner child can help us understand our adult experience. The problem with childhood trauma is that, when left untreated, it's hard to be happy. A feeling of impending doom and lack of safety is constantly throbbing below the surface.

Luckily, we can overcome this feeling. By doing inner child work, we can heal our wounds and become happy, successful, and joyful people. First, though, we need to take a good, long look at our wounds and figure out why they are keeping us stuck.

<u>Prompts: The wounds that keep you stuck</u>   (Get Unstuck! paperback edition page 261)

Friendly reminder: I'm not a therapist, psychologist, or healthcare professional. I'm a coach. If you have severe trauma, attachment, or childhood wounds or need medical support, please get in touch with a healthcare professional. I've added a list of organizations that can help at the end of this book.

For this exercise, I want you to (re)connect with your inner child. You don't need to write anything down if you don't feel like it, but writing is the best way to connect on a deeper level with yourself. Find a quiet spot to sit or lay down. Once you've read through the questions, start writing or close your eyes and ponder:

- **How was I as a child?**
- **What is my happiest childhood memory? My wildest dream?**
- **Were there any decisive events that shaped how I see the world today?**
- **How does my inner child see the world?**
- **What beliefs about the world started in my childhood for me?**
- **When I was a child, what did I want to be when I grew up?**
- **What's a funny yet embarrassing moment from my childhood?**
- **What is my inner child saying to me today?**
- **What does my inner child need from me today?**
- **How will I give my inner child the love and support I wanted as a child?**
- **What is one step I can take to get unstuck?**

To truly overcome our childhood wounds and trauma, we need to build a more secure attachment with ourselves. We must recognize that we always have our own backs – we will never abandon ourselves. By realizing this, we can start to shift our lives, gaining confidence, and moving towards the reality we want to experience. The exercise below will help you learn how to do this.

Prompt: How can I build a more secure attachment with myself?
(Get Unstuck! paperback edition page 271)

Imagine someone you'd feel secure being around. Someone that has your back no matter what and who supports you while giving you the freedom to explore the world. Maybe you have someone like that in your life; in that case, think of them.

Now think about how this person shows up for you. What do they do when you need help? When you're sad? When you feel lonely or misunderstood? How do they help you navigate difficult situations? What do they do when something great happens in your life? How do they celebrate with you? What happens when you don't speak to them for a while or when you're busy with your life?

For each aspect below, reflect on how the person you've imagined above would embody them. Then, modeling them, imagine how you can give more of these things to yourself.

- **Being present with yourself.**
- **Loving yourself.**
- **Trusting yourself.**
- **Being compassionate towards yourself.**
- **Living a values-based life.**
- **Changing your mindset.**
- **Living in integrity with yourself.**
- **Committing to yourself daily.**
- **Being fiercely disciplined in your growth journey.**

....

....

....

....

....

....

....

Finally, ask yourself what you need to feel more securely attached to yourself. What is the one thing you can start doing right now? Then commit to doing it.

CHAPTER 5: THE MOST EFFECTIVE WAY TO DO SOMETHING, IS TO DO IT.

One of the things that many people have a hard time with is finding the one thing that will keep them inspired and going forward. Creatives and entrepreneurs (not to mention creative generalists) can have difficulty knowing what to focus on – they simply have too many ideas.

People feel stuck, ashamed even, for not having a clear higher purpose, a reason outside themselves for why they want to do what they do. We have to find our unique glue – our reason for why we want to do what we do.

The clearer you get about your glue, the easier it become to choose what to focus on and eventually make progress on your goals.

<u>Prompt: What's your glue?</u>   (Get Unstuck! paperback edition page 276)

What unique theme or common thread makes everything come together and make sense for you?
The questions below will help you identify your main theme. Don't despair if you can't pinpoint one clear thing; a sense of what that theme might be for you is good enough to get you started. As you progress on your journey of self-discovery, and as you live more and more aligned with your values and authentic self, your glue will continue to manifest itself.

- **When are you the happiest?**
- **What activities quickly get you into flow?**
- **What makes you come alive?**
- **What topics interest you the most?**
- **What type of work do you like to do?**
- **What motivates you to keep going?**
- **What's your most secret dream?**
- **When do you get to use your entire skillset?**
- **What do you enjoy doing?**
- **What keeps you interested and gives you energy?**

Look at your answers to the questions above and try to distill a common theme or thread from them. What are the reasons why you do what you do? What's the number one thing that makes you feel alive?

Now that we know what our glue is, it's time to choose something to get started with – the thing you know you really want the most right now.

<u>Prompt: The thing I'm going to get started with is...</u>   (Get Unstuck! paperback edition page 278)

Review the "What do you really want?" exercises if you need to, and when you're ready, focus on the one thing you want to get started with. I'm not asking you to dismiss anything if you have many things you want to do; just choose one that you'll get started with right now. Write it down as a positive mantra and put it where you can see it daily.

....

....

....

....

....

....

....

Here's the example of Martha, a client stuck in a demanding job that left no room for any creative pursuits,
who realized she wanted to go back to theater after having enjoyed it so much as a child.

"Enroll in acting class at my local community center so I can step on stage and feel alive again."

Or take Hamza's example, who felt stuck in his final year of college and was pressured by his parents to attend medical school. Hamza could only see the pile of debt he was amassing and the years spent studying for a career he knew wasn't his dream but his parents'. After a few sessions of digging deep into what Hamza wanted, here's what came up:

"Build the courage to follow my dream of becoming a documentary maker, and get the funding I need for my first project about young entrepreneurs and their impact on creating sustainable communities."

In Get Unstuck! we've learned why we get stuck, what is keeping us stuck, and what we want to do once we get unstuck. But how do we stay unstuck? There are three things we can do to make sure we stay in motion and continue working towards our dreams:

1. Consistency is key – don't break the chain.
2. Cultivate a state of flow.
3. Don't make one thing the focus of your life.

<u>**Final prompt: Set a goal, the first one you'll take on when you're done reading this book.**</u>
(Get Unstuck! paperback edition page 291)

Ask yourself for the last time what you want, but this time take all the knowledge of this book with you in your answer. Be as honest and truthful with yourself as possible. Then follow the steps below, one by one.

What do you really want?

- State a clear goal for yourself.
- List the reasons you want to achieve this goal (what will it bring to your life?).
- Are you setting this goal from your wounds, other people's dreams, or what you think you must do? Or are you wanting this from a place of freedom and joy (the right place)?
- Reflect on who you need to be(come) to achieve your goal. What shoes do you need to fill?
- List the steps you need to take to reach your goal in terms of doing and being.
- Make a list of the positive habits and rituals you will cultivate to achieve this goal.
- Reflect on what negative hurdles your environment might place in your way and devise ways to change your environment to help you accomplish your goals.
- Make a top three of the ways you're going to stay consistent in working toward this goal. How will you harness the power of the compound effect?
- By when do you want to achieve this goal?
- Buy a calendar (or use the universal one provided in the workbook to this book), circle the day you've defined in the previous step, and hang the calendar on a wall somewhere visible.
- Take one step today towards your goal, and mark this day on your calendar with an X.
- Do the same tomorrow, and mark that day with another X.
- Don't break the chain.

I'm so proud of you for making it to this point. I know it wasn't easy. I asked you so many questions and wouldn't let you off the hook. But you did it, and now you're ready. I can't wait to see all the beautiful things you're going to create and the amazing life that awaits you.

I believe in you. **Now get up and get unstuck.**

PS: Please, don't leave me in the dark, I'd love to know what your goal is and how you're doing! Send me a message on Instagram @muriellemarie or email me directly at murielle@muriellemarie.com.

Murielle Marie xoxo